For Aileen, Zara and
Especially for Colin ~~because~~
publisher, connected with the Church.
With love, Keith.

TIMES AND SEASONS

A calendar of poems and reflections

Sheena Munro   2014

TIMES AND SEASONS

EPIPHANY

Out of the eastern night they came,

Knowing the dangers, powerless to resist

The strange compulsion of the foreign star

That blazed ahead of them.

What did they hope to find?

A king, yes, to be hailed with gold –

That much they understood.

But what of the other gifts whose names they read

In the cold enigmatic galaxies?

Frankincense for a new, all-powerful God?

Their books, like the stars, told them of gods without number.

What was so special in this one, to bring them searching

The land of the Jews?

And - most mysterious – myrrh, the herb of death:

Could they have understood this one aright?

A birth – and a death?

Or many deaths – a terrifying start

For a new regime. But so it had to be.

CANDLEMAS, The snowdrop

A spear of white, a tiny flame of hope

Piercing the winter night with tenderness.

The night flows, chill and deep, filling the heart

With aching loneliness; blindly, the soul

Searches for freedom from its choking bonds;

But where? And suddenly, a distant spark

Gleams – hold fast, eyes, this is no mere illusion;

This is the flame of love that will not die,

That, fanned by hope, can never be extinguished.

The light grows into glory, and we learn

With stumbling steps to walk in it, and know

The joy of fellowship with Him, in whom

There is no darkness, only light eternal.

LENT slideshow

Hopeful green haze on wind-scoured fields

Pale crocus lances challenging the chillness

A purr of catkins peeping through willow twigs

Hawthorn buds pricking winter-honed branches

Gorse ablaze with gold through its crown of thorns

Tiny irises among drifts of snowdrops

Bearing their purple message of peace

Camellia, promising the roses of summer

An early triumphant fanfare of daffodils –

The lovely pain of spring

THE COMING

When I went to draw water –

That was when he came.

I had lingered at the well, dreaming a while

Of how it would be when I was married, a mother.

They had chosen a husband for me – Joseph the carpenter,

A good man, they told me, hard-working, honest and kind.

But as I gazed into the sunlit water

I saw the face of Another, grave and radiant.

I turned to apologise for keeping him waiting

and he greeted me: *hail, thou that art highly favoured.*

I tried to speak, but my tongue would not make the words

And I thought I was dreaming still as he talked of a Child…

I stammered at last that there must be some mistake,

I wasn't married – how could this be for me?

And he told me – o wonder too powerful to believe –

That the Lord's own spirit would father this child on me,

The Child who would be our nation's long-promised Saviour.

As I raised my head and looked into his eyes,

I felt my terror silently slide away

And I knew that the Lord had taken me into His care

And that all would be as the glorious stranger had said.

He melted back into the summer sunshine

And I thought I heard a swell of heavenly music

That filled my soul with a glory of hope and praise.

I WAS THERE

Yes, I was there in the crowd
That heady spring afternoon on the Mount of Olives
When the word went round the city: *See, He is coming,*
The King is coming, riding on the back of a donkey
Just as the prophet foretold. O the joy of that day,
The dreams that flared into hope in men's eager eyes!
And the bright blue sky was full of psalms and hosannas.
Little Reuben tugged at my sleeve and asked *Abba, why?*
And I told him excitedly of the long-promised Messiah,
And he laughed and waved his palm branch and shouted
Hosanna!
And I whispered a prayer – *Lord, is it time at last?*

We talked of Him as we prepared for Passover
When already the doubts were gathering in men's eyes;
Not the women – they spoke of gentleness and compassion,
Of the hands that healed; but the men were shaking their
heads
And labelling him a weakling, a friend of the Romans
Who said we should pay our taxes, do what we were told.
And when little Reuben asked the traditional question:
WHY? Why is this night unlike any other?
We told all the painful story of our people
And I saw in my mind the doors marked with crosses of
blood.

I was there on the street they now call *Dolorosa*
And they told me how the crowd shouted *We want
Barabbas!*
And *Crucify him!* And I felt my heart freeze within me
When little Reuben tearfully whispered *WHY?*
Abba, why do they want to kill the King?
A weeping Judean rushed past us, clutching a bag
Of money to his chest. His face still haunts my dreams.
The storm broke that afternoon and raged all night
And I prayed in anguish: *Lord, what have we done?*
I still don't know, but one thing I do remember:
The glorious sunshine the morning after Sabbath
And a woman running, shouting : *The Lord is risen!*

'Early on the first day of the week, while it was still dark...'

Hope lay imprisoned in the silent darkness.
Grief ceased its roaring, and the shuddering sobs
At last grew quiet; weary hands and feet
Dragged themselves into their accustomed tasks.
The garden slept still; the unguarded tomb
Stood empty, and they did not understand.

A sliver of gold slit the reluctant sky;
the light of life anointed her bowed head,
streamed all around and over her, and love
filled all the place with fragrance.
The day shone out in glorious radiance
And hope broke from its prison.

MARY

I cradled him

Watched as he grew and played and jumped and ran

Among the sun-bleached stones; and when he fell

I bathed the grazed knees, soothed them with a kiss.

I watched him die,

Prayed for the awful agony to end;

And when they took his broken body down,

I held him one more time against my heart:

My dear, dead Son.

MAGDALENE

I followed him,

Those last long weeks, along the dusty roads;

I bathed his feet, anointing him with perfume

And wiped them with my hair: they called me mad.

I watched him die;

Went to the tomb to do him one last service

And found his body gone; then through my tears

I saw him once again in radiant glory:

My risen Lord.

THREE CROSSES

St John the Evangelist remembers
Three crosses, black against the mourning sky,
Branded forever on my memory.
His Mother, leaning on me, faint with weeping.
'Mother' He spoke, commending her to me
And me to her from that day on, to be
Together always, working for the Word
That now returned to God. We saw him yield
His spirit up, heard his departing words.

Here, in my rocky prison
The burning sun traces its daily path
Across the floor, as I strive to record
His teaching; and my weary eyes, grown dim
With writing, peer into the dazzling cleft
That brings me light, and even now I see them,
Those three stark crosses etched against the sky.

He too was closed up in a silent cave
Until the woman came to us that morning
To tell us he was gone. With bursting lungs
I ran, and flung myself into the tomb,
Saw, and believed, and when I came outside
And raised my eyes to heaven – seeking him?
I know not, but against the blazing sky
I saw them standing still on Golgotha,
Those three, bare, empty crosses.

PENTECOST

Back in the homely calm of Galilee
They worked and talked, soothing the lingering pain
After He left them. Here, where their hearts had thrilled
At His first teachings, now they waited, wondering
At this, His last commission: *Feed my sheep*
Out on those grassy hills above the lake
Where they had watched Him feed the hungry thousands,
They prayed at sunset, seeking as He had done
To know the Father's will.

And so the time came when they said farewell
Again to Galilee, turning their steps
Back to Jerusalem. Their hearts were full
As they walked once again the ancient streets
That rang with recent, awful memories.
They saw averted eyes, heard mutterings,
But knew the time had come to bring the message
The promise of the long-awaited freedom.

Holiday crowds pressed noisily around them,

Curious, hostile, mocking, eager, longing.

So Peter spoke, and a great silence fell

Upon the listeners, and then there came

A mighty rushing wind, and flickering flames

That did not burn, yet fired the wondering spirits

With a strange longing, and the deepening knowledge

That now the time had come.

PENTECOST PRAYER

Spirit of Love, waken our sleeping hearts,
Kindle in us your purifying fire,
Consuming envy, anger and mistrust,
Moving us to reach out in fellowship
And hand in hand to come in faith together
Into the loving presence of our Lord.

Spirit of Joy, sing in our silent minds,
Teach us to raise our voices in His praise,
Open our eyes to His magnificence,
Lead us as we rejoice in His great goodness,
Sending our hymn of hope and gladness soaring
Into the radiant presence of our Lord.

Spirit of Peace, enfold our restless souls,
Soothing and healing, comforting our pain,
Banishing troubled thoughts and dark despair:
Let us in stillness and serenity
Bring all our sorrows and anxieties
Into the saving presence of our Lord.

SPIRIT GIFTS

Spirit of Love, fill our uncaring hearts,
Help us to love one another for His sake.
Spirit of Joy, sing through our halting praise
And help us to rejoice in Him.
Spirit of Peace, soothe our tempestuous souls
And bring us quietness.
Spirit of Patience, teach us how to wait
And know His time.
Spirit of Kindness, keep our hands and mouths
From doing harm to any of His creatures.
Spirit of Goodness, guard our minds from evil,
That we may strive to follow His example.
Spirit of Faithfulness, strengthen weak resolve
And keep our wavering eyes fixed on His cross.
Spirit of Gentleness, comfort the distressed
And make them mindful of His boundless love.
Spirit of Self-control, grant that the *self*
Be lost forever in His holy service.

SUMMER: WAITING

Swifts overhead –

the ceaseless, restless quest for food, for life.

Clouds shifting endlessly, majestic

Across the mountain face, veiling from view

The massive crenellated summit.

'I will lift up my eyes to the hills:

Whence comes my aid?'

- not from those frowning unrelenting strongholds

that ring my soul around, imprisoning

the wings of hope, of truth.

But I must wait in patience till the sun

Breaks through in healing warmth and peace- and look!

The clouds part, and the gracious blue of heaven

beckons behind the fortress, and the way

shines clear, and on the wings of truth I soar.

MIDSUMMER : the feast of St John

Flickering in the shortness of the night,
The flames of love unfold.
The longing hearts meet in a surge of joy
And recognition.
The fire-rose blooms, petals of crimson whirl
Around love's beacon, and the sweet-sad thrill
Of singing from the unseen nightingale
Rings out in blessing.

This is Love's feast: now they join hand in hand
To leap the dying embers.
So love and loyalty unite, for ever
Pledging devotion.
Together now, they watch the fire-smoke curl
Bearing their prayers, and their glad hearts fill
With hope, as the dawn whispers, silvery pale
A breeze of blessing.

SEASONS

See, I have placed My rainbow in the heavens,

you who are always asking for a SIGN

only look up, when eyes are dulled with tears

and every hope seems lost – do you remember?

I promised, I the Lord of all Creation

seed-time and harvest, while the earth remains.

I gave this to you, this, My work of Love;

I ask this only, stay true to that Love,

tend it with care, respect its every need,

Hold to My Covenant!

SUMMER PILGRIMAGE

This road surely has no end!

I stutter from one passing place to another – always

another car coming towards me:

strangers who don't know the code.

Returning Iona pilgrims?

Pilgrimages don't end at the holy site –

that is where they begin.

By the road, the dykestones catch my eye –

Patterns of light and colour leaping out

With a new brightness.

Stones washed by the rain,

Water that searches and smoothes

sculpting the life within,

life that shines out into the waiting light.

Follow the living stones that light the way

To new discovery.

SAVING GRACE

They waited, huddled on the unkind rocks
Outside the town, under the merciless sun.
On filthy stinking rags the bloated flies
Crawled over wasted limbs, tormenting legs
That once had freely walked and run and climbed,
Lips that had smiled, eyes that had shone with youth.

Shunned by the world, sharing the bread of pain.
The wine of bitterness, they waited there
For him to pass, hope scarcely daring yet
To creep into the sad, cold, suffering souls.
He came; they clamoured : *Master, pity us!*

Love and compassion flooded from his eyes;
The tingling, burning life came surging back;
The tortured flesh grew whole and firm again.
Go to the priest and show yourselves – they walked

Then ran and jumped, embracing, yelled

With unbelieving joy. He watched them go,

And waited….Back along the sun-baked road

One figure came at last to kneel before him.

I thank you, Master. Gently powerful hands

Rested in blessing on the matted hair,

Embraced him, gently raised him up. *Are you*

The only one, you, the Samaritan?

Go now in peace, your faith has made you whole.

LAMMAS: the season of fruit

Now is the time of bearing fruit: the earth

Swells joyfully, and gladly now brings forth

Its sweet love-offerings. The amber dews

Distilling in the hearts of flowers, join

In their deep alchemy. As summer spills

Into the gold of autumn, song and laughter

Celebrate harvest.

HARVEST

This is the time for taking stock,

For gathering in the fruits of labour,

For clearing away the debris of summer's exuberance,

For separating the grain from the chaff,

For filling the storehouses against the coming winter,

For offering up the first, the best, the sweetest,

For taking the bread and the wine,

For making new beginnings.

For giving thanks.

FLOWER SERVICE

My turn to do the flowers: in the silence
Peace reaches out, enfolds me as I work.
The glory of creation blazes here,
Crimson and golden, purple, white and blue,
A silken spectrum curls among my fingers,
Glowing reminder of the covenant promise.

What of our part? Surrounded as we are
By beauty, what a sad imperfect world
We offer in return! These glossy leaves
And pliant stems show forth the heritage
Of health and vigour that is ours to share –
But to our shame, how little we deserve.

Fragrance surrounds me, rising like a prayer.
My gentle task is done. I thank you, Lord.

AUTUMN PALETTE

Dahlia, marigold, nasturtium –

Glorious tapestry in blazing golds;

Harvest fields rolling out to the blue horizon;

Scarlet berries of rosehip and rowan:

Rich store for the winter to come;

Sunlight slanting through trees glowing amber and crimson;

Harvest moon hanging low in the indigo heaven;

Scatter of starfire shimmering in the first frost;

Rainbow's promise arching through the clouds –

Pictures that shine in the mind as the year grows darker

Pointing us forward to the sun's return.

The plangent calls of geese and curlew ring

Across the frosty fields, as the earth sinks

Quietly into its dark winter dream

Of new beginnings, rest and preparation.

Deep in earth's womb, the cycle still continues.

MAGNOLIAS AT THE CHURCH WINDOW

Elegant tracery of ancient stone

Guarding the light of the Creator Spirit –

This is His home, here where the squalid lusts

And dark preoccupations of the world

May not intrude: a righteous barrier

Darkly excludes the meek, the poor in spirit

Who long to know Him.

Blest are the pure in heart, whose fragile strength

Spears upward, the integrity of hope

Wearing the white of mourning for a world

Betrayed and fallen: tenderness and peace,

Loving, forgiving, reconciling.

CHRISTMAS CARDS

There are gaudy cardboard boxes

Filled with perfumes, silks and toys;

There are mince pies and punch for the carollers

And cheerful Christmas noise;

There are wide-eyed children playing the parts

Of shepherds and wise men three

And gifts from the family marked 'with love'

Hanging on the tree.

There are battered cardboard boxes

With people sleeping inside;

There are starving families huddled in tents

On a desolate mountainside;

There are terrified children with shattered limbs

In countries still not free

And the Father's precious gift of Love

Hanging on a tree.

NO ROOM

No room tonight, I'm afraid; you'll have to be on your way.

Bethlehem just isn't big enough for all the house of David.

No good complaining to me: this census wasn't my idea.

Well, of course I'll make money out of it – it's my livelihood.

What's that you say – all the way from Nazareth

And your wife's about to give birth? Well, I'm sorry

But all the rooms have been taken by Roman soldiers

And it's more than my life's worth to cross any of *them*.

Look, I'll tell you what, seeing as how you're desperate,

I can let the two of you bed down in the stable.

It's warm in there, the beasts'll not bother you

And there's plenty of clean straw – well. It's the best I can do

And I'll only charge half price – well, I've got to make a living...

No time to read all this charity stuff – don't they know it's Christmas?

I've the cards to get and write, and no presents bought yet.

No point in sending appeals when money's so tight,

And I haven't ordered the turkey or the wine;

I've the kids to take to see Santa, and Ben wants new trainers

And Emma'll need a new dress for the Sunday School party.

What's that, they're dying of hunger in Africa?

46

Yes, it's terrible, isn't it – I saw it on the telly.

But I mean, what difference can I make? It's the Government's job

To see to things like that – we pay taxes, don't we?

Look, I really don't have time, I'm off to town,

But I'll get those charity Christmas cards – that'll help, won't it?

No change, I'm afraid; I'll need this for the car park

And we've spent a small fortune today – you should see the prices.

No use going back to the hole in the wall either;

We've used up all we had saved, and a bit beside.

What's that? Yes, it has turned cold, hasn't it?

You must be frozen, standing here on this street corner.

We might have snow tonight – well, it'd be seasonal

And nice for the kids to get out and do some sledging

And give us some peace. It's a real hassle, isn't it,

Christmas? It wasn't always like this, was it?

Armies of occupation, children dying,

Families driven out to live in caves,

No room...no time...no change.

EMMANUEL – GOD WITH US

The year sinks down into darkness,

Huddled against the penetrating frost,

Finger-numbing, bone-aching cold.

The day wakes late and drags itself grumpily

Through its few shivery grey hours

Till chilly night enshrouds the world again.

Kindle the fires of love! Blow healing warmth

Into the sad cold hearts.

Lift up your eyes and see where in the east

A star is shining.

A CHILD IS BORN

Exhausted, exalted,

She gazed on the tiny face of her sleeping child.

Her husband smoothed her dark, damp hair.

You did well, lass. You should sleep now.

Smiling, she shook her head.

I can't close my eyes. I have to watch over him.

Imagine, Joseph, he's ours now to look after

Until he grows up, the Lord of all creation.

Joseph stretched out his hand, a joiner's hand,

The skin roughened and hacked from years of work;

A gentle pinkie touched the peach-soft cheek

And the baby Lord made a small soft sound of blessing.

Mary never told Joseph

Of the pain that seared her heart.

Listen, love! she murmured, *the sky is full of singing.*

NATIVITY

Who is this, lying in a bed of straw

Under the shadow of an unsheathed sword?

Drawing first human breath, here in a stable,

This is the Resurrection and the Life.

Who is this, whom philosophers and shepherds

Leaving their books and flocks, hasten to worship,

Guided by star and angel? In this stable

This is the Way, the Truth, the Life.

Who is this sleeping in the whispering darkness,

Lulled by the loving murmurs of his mother,

Warmed by the breath of beasts? Here in the stable,

This is the Light of the world.

AND THE LIGHT SHINETH IN DARKNESS,
AND THE DARKNESS COMPREHENDED IT NOT

The night is cold and dark,

Weary and slow the travellers

Painfully trudging the pitiless miles of a journey

That started, it seems, at the beginning of time

And still no end in sight.

How far IS it to Bethlehem?

And is that really where we want to go?

Our hearts were so full of hope at the beginning,

But the way is so long and so hard

And the eyes of those we meet are full of suspicion

And their hearts are full of darkness and of hate.

We search for the One who will give us all the answers,

Who will lead us out of this world of darkness and nightmare

Where evil twists the soul, and love is stifled.

But how much longer can we go on searching?

Did our dreams tell us lies, were our hopes a mere illusion?

Must it go on forever, this dark and painful journey?

Look up, travellers.

Raise your eyes heavenwards, see where the star shines still.

Your eyes have been clouded by human history,

But still the star is there, still it draws us in hope

To the source of the true, the everlasting light

That shines in the eyes of a Child.

EPILOGUE

Thank you, Lord, for words,

For the gifts of listening ,speaking, writing

of hearing in our hearts the still small voice

that speaks the infinite wonder of your Creation

of opening ears and minds to listen and learn

and echo your truths that shine there;

of sharing praise, questions, epiphanies;

of bringing to you our thoughts.